Chalice of Tears

Chalice of Tears

Poems by

Karin Temple

Radiolarian Press
Astoria, Oregon

Radiolarian Press
92673 John Day River Road
Astoria, Oregon 97103

First edition

ISBN 978-1-887853-41-5

The following poems have appeared previously, sometimes in different form:

Time Travel; September 1, 1939; The Allure of Potato Pancakes; "The Mail from Tunis, probably" in *RAIN* (Astoria, Oregon).

Destination Prague in *StringTown* (Spokane, Washington).

1941 in *Child of War* (StringTown Press, Spokane).

Photographs of Charles Schweigert's art by Andrew Cier.

für Mutti und Tata

Contents

The Petrified Angel

The Holiness of Broken Things

The Petrified Angel

Maikäfer flieg!
Dein Vater ist im Krieg,
deine Mutter ist in Pommerland,
Pommerland ist abgebrannt,
Maikäfer flieg!

Des Knaben Wunderhorn, 1808

May beetle, fly far!
Your father is in the war,
your mother is in Baltic lands,
Baltic lands went up in flames,
May beetle, fly far!

German children's song (trans. Karin Temple)

Time Travel

Today's trains
      silent
      sleek
hurry through
the homeland
blur names
of small stations
make hasty stops
in large cities.

      Consider
the emergency brake
to still the image
of a gently flowing river
a field with poppies
shining slate roofs.

Only the tunnels
      deep
      and blind
have saved
the black echoes
the thick smell of soot
from once-upon-a-time
steam locomotives
chugging and puffing
      never again
      never again
      never again.

September 1, 1939

On the tram ride home
from her shift at
the textile mill,
worried-looking men
and women whisper
or stare ahead.
At the corner kiosk
the mute screaming
of black headlines.
She does not stop
to buy a paper and
is glad to shut doors
behind her, house door,
apartment door,
the door to her sublet room.
Numb, she sits
on her narrow bed.
The Führer's frenzied voice
from the landlady's
radio is omnipresent
in every household of
the city, the country.
She can't quite
understand the words,
but she cannot escape
the voice. When the speech
is over, she slowly chews
her supper of rye bread,
sausage, and cheese,
then washes stockings
and underwear in the sink.
And goes to bed in
the hushed house.

Mother, they are still
announcing war
over the radio.
The child you begat
a year later at Christmas
on the Polish front with
one of the conquering
soldiers, that child
is old now and curses
a world where
tanks still roll
and bullets and bombs
still kill.

1941

Two women
search the towering crowd
amidst steam and scream
of locomotives,
drone of loudspeakers,
piercing whistle signals,
doors slamming, wheels gaining speed.
After bustling bodies
have drained into exits
their eyes lock
their lives lock
they savor the slow approach:
one with a jaunty hat
on soft curls,
little girl feet in high heels,
her gravity showing;
the other, thick graying hair
in a bun,
has only shortly
left the fixing
of the welcome meal,
breathless in her apron
she presents the flowers
seizes the suitcase
and arm in arm
they fall into step.
They will be bombed and conquered
shamed and evicted
they will cook stone soup
wear widows' black

while tenderly
raising the child together
invincible.
I am circled
in their first embrace.

Spoils of War
or What did the soldier's wife get?

after Bertolt Brecht

From Poland she got
the fat Christmas goose
a famous Polish goose
for that first Christmas
without him.

From Narvik he sent
the glossiest fur muff
soft Northern mink
for warming her hands—
that's what she got from Norway.

From Brussels she got
a collar of lace
precious bobbin lace
to flatter her face—
that's what he sent from Belgium.

From Paris she got
a delightful little hat
an elegant chapeau
with a tilt so chic—
that's what he sent from the city of lights.

From Rumania she got
the blue peasant blouse
an embroidered blouse
too foreign to wear—
that's what she got from Bucharest.

From Sofia he sent
a small icon of gold
of a stern-looking saint
with emblems so strange—
that's what she got from Bulgaria.

And what did the soldier's wife get
from the Russian front?
From Russia she got
the widow's veil
the black widow's veil
from Stalingrad.

Sustenance

Gardens were a given during the hard times—
vegetables, dill and parsley, a few rows
of asters and sweet peas along the fence
grew in every backyard. Bicyclists, balancing
a rake or a spade on their way to an outlying
Schrebergarten, were a common sight. Fridays,
when the fishmonger's cart loaded with plaice
came through, eager gardeners watched, pail
in hand, and hurried to collect steaming
horseapples for their tomato plants.

Gardens were also for giving—
nobody but my mother chided me for picking
a handful of berries, a ripe pear, or a flower
out of a neighbor's yard. Overabundant produce
would find its way to our doorstep, green
beans, peas, cucumbers in summer, frosted kale
or Brussels sprouts in winter.

Gardens not only helped us survive but secretly
connected us to other distressed parts of
the world by a web of underground roots like
far-reaching mushroom mycelia.
Victory gardens in England and America,
ghetto gardens in Poland,
prisoner-of-war gardens
even in Russia, pictured
in two watercolors my father brought back.
Japanese internees landscaped the barren
desert camps of California, raked paths
and rocks defining raised beds, ponds,
the occasional tree.

All these war and post-war gardens
had one thing in common: they transformed
the most basic human need for growing food
into an act of defiance, a symbol of hope,
a manifesto of beauty, a prayer for peace.

Watercolor by Willi Silz (1947) titled "Lagergarten" (camp garden) depicting a
prisoner-of-war garden created by Stalingrad survivors.

Rosemary for Remembrance

Ophelia, Hamlet, *Act 4, Scene 5*

"There's rosemary, that's for remembrance"
There's chamomile, that's for healing
There's beeswax candles, that's for holiness
There's sweet peas, that's for happiness
There's books, that's for adventure
There's codliver oil, that's for strength
There's *Nivea Creme,* that's for soothing
There's spiders, that's for fright
There's airdried sheets, that's for ease
There's roast pork, that's for satisfaction
There's rye bread, that's for sustenance
There's poppyseed stollen, that's for love
There's four-leaf clover, that's for luck
"There's rue for you; and here's some for me."

Blacklisted

Sugar beets were a major crop
in our region. The flat fields
of Lower Saxony apportioned by
tree-lined roads and rows
of shiny beet greens. The town
had a sugar factory suffusing
the air with treacly smells
in the fall. The same smell
escaped from a cellar where
women were gathered to scrub
and cut up heaps of white beets
for boiling in a large copper
kettle, taking turns stirring
until the simmering mass
in the cauldron was reduced
to night-black molasses we used
to spread on rye bread.
As a child, I was a wide-eyed
witness to the subterranean
toil, the heat, the sweat,
the banter, the fingerlicking
sweet stickiness.
As a young woman, when I was
passionate about farming for
subsistence, I asked my Tata
how to make this *Rübenkraut*.
She refused.
She had always granted me
every wish, cooked, baked, knit
what I requested.

During my new life overseas,
she sent her secret recipes
on diaphanous airmail
stationery, instructions for
headcheese, pickles, sauerkraut.
This time only, she wrote
"Nein. No one should have
to do that ever again."
She never explained and I never asked. So
I ended up feeding my beet harvest
to the pigs.

Mother Tongue

A window swings open
the mother leans forward
calling out loud
    Ischi, Ischi!
calling her child in
from play from danger
of approaching dark.
Oh for that name
      that voice
      that readiness
to run home toward
her wide-open arms!

Destination Prague

Between the window's
double wings
I lean out
to feel how fresh
the breeze
from the Moldau;
drab Žitna Street
yawns below
deserted
in the morning grey
of Jan Hus Day.

The whispering voice
of a young woman
tells secrets
of Old-New Synagogue:
the five-ribbed
Gothic vault.
The small window
for catching
the first light of dawn.
The seat of Rabbi Loew.
      Of Pinkas Synagogue
I remember nothing
but the names on the walls,
the names, in small
script to fit all,
the endless procession
of last name, first name,
date of deportation,
last name, first name,
date of deportation,

seventy-seven thousand names
silently
accusing me.

In Strašnice Cemetery
rows of orderly tombstones
rise from a sea of ivy
to curse their gold German script.
The grave of
Dr. Franz Kafka
can be found
close to the wall
at the intersection of
two numbers where
he lies trapped
in the claws of Prague
and the company
of his parents
under a heavy
marker in Hebrew.
The sisters,
Elli, Valli, and Ottla,
graveless, their names
on a small pillow of granite.

Coming from a town
of soft sliding hills
with wooden houses
eager to decay
I marvel
at the stony solidity
of this sorrowful city.
Only stones
could outlast
the countless woes—

18

occupation, reformation,
defenestration, deportation,
protestation, and separation;
the rock promontory
of the Vyšehrad,
the tall walls and steps
of Hradčany Castle,
the masonry of bridges,
churches, and houses,
the gravestones, even
the lowly cobblestones,
wet on a July night,
speak of the firm
determination
to endure.

Soup for Some

Two women working a soup kitchen
in a war-busy train station,
all in frantic motion
of arrival and departure,
soldiers leaving for the front,
soldiers on furlough,
refugees with large bundles,
travelers with suitcases.

A freight train stands on a side rail.

The women ladle out soup for the hungry,
for the uniformed, the civilians,
ladle pea soup, wash tin bowls,
dole out more soup.
During a lull between trains
they rest their aching arms
and notice faint noises
from the boxcars—voices?

The pair get busy again,
continue their patriotic ladling
of soup convincing each other
that they heard nothing.

A few years later they must acknowledge
what it was they could have known,
must acknowledge that they were ladling
and ladling in the seventh circle of Hell.

Displaced

In June, my water heater sprang a leak
and I spent a week at the Comfort Inn
during repairs to the kitchen floor.
This was the third time in my life
that I had been displaced.

The first time, it was bombs and I was
an infant. The second time was an eviction
by the American Military because of
my uncle's prominent position in the
National Socialist Party.

I was four when we were assigned
to a one-family villa together with
refugees from the East. The owner
and life-long resident of the house
had to share the upstairs with
a refugee from Lithuania who became
my fearsome elementary school teacher.
The floor the two women occupied
was separated from us by a beautiful
wooden staircase with bannisters
and a stained-glass window at the bend.
They had their own kitchen and toilet.

My mother and aunt and I were allotted
two downstairs rooms connected by
French doors, a kitchen with running
cold water plus a pantry, and cellar
storage. These quarters grew crowded
when my uncle returned from prison
and my father from Stalingrad.

An extra room on our floor was occupied
by an older woman and her adult son,
a cellar compartment by a woman with
two unruly teen-age sons, all of them
refugees from East Prussia. There was
one toilet and no bath.

The insurance company placed me
in a suite. I had two TVs, a kitchen,
a sitting room, a king-sized bed,
and a bathroom with shower and tub.
This week of comfortable temporary exile
caused by an insignificant domestic
disaster nevertheless triggered
that old ever-ready child-of-war affliction
which I numbed by watching Turner movies,
propped up by a multitude of pillows
in the middle of the huge bed.

Transformation

Take an empty space.
A large empty space,
like a gym. With
basketball hoops,
a noisy heater, posters
pitching milk. With
a security lock system
and a barred equipment room.
A gym in a prison.

A guard lets in two women with
the basic ingredients
to a planned activity:
a heavy, folded canvas cloth,
battery candles,
recorded chants.
And the ceremony of unfolding
takes place, revealing
turn by turn
the ancient geometry
of the labyrinth,
purple pattern on white.
The women walk the circumference
holding and lifting hands
in waves of blessing.

Now the guard brings in
seven young men in prison grey,
single file, orders them
to line up against the wall
and take off their shoes.

The women greet them,
eye to eye, hand to hand,
exchanging names, and gesture
to sit with them on the floor
forming a circle.
They talk about the strangely
winding path of the labyrinth,
the path of life, about direction
and detours, meaning and mystery,
trust.

Each at their own time
and pace, seven men
and one of the women
enter the labyrinth
and abandon themselves to
the circling and turning,
meeting and parting,
standing still, beginning again
on the path to the center,
pilgrims,
alone and together
on a slow and quiet journey
of remembrance and regret,
of prayer and hope.

Come and see:
they reach up to heaven,
they bow down humbly,
one twirls in the middle
of the crowded rose petal
center. Then they retrace
their steps, still unhurried
and reverent, one boy
walking backwards.

Emerging from the labyrinth,
words are whispered of
calm and peace,
of childhood,
of failings, discoveries,
and resolves.

This miracle
is repeated with
four more groups
of seven troubled youths
who enter their prison gym
and encounter
a sacred space
full of grace.
On their knees,
the last seven help
the two women roll up
the large canvas, turn
by turn secreting
the sacred pattern
anew.

"The Mail from Tunis, probably"

Emily Dickinson

At elevenses
the mailman comes

my messenger
in celestial blue

my Hermes
in pith helmet

impersonating humanness
by a penchant for gossip

he makes his fateful
steady rounds

equanimous
to the nature of the news

the black-rimmed letter
the gaudy card the bill

his heaviest burden
the glossy hymns of commerce

his prize (and mine)
the post from overseas

as light and bright
as plumage

all gently placed
but with finality

of metal
slapping shut.

One day, messages
hand-written
hand-delivered
will go the way to Hades

like the telegraph boy
on his bicycle

like the herald
with shoes and helmet winged—

not yet, Olympians, not yet!

The Allure of Potato Pancakes

Potatoes and grease,
it's that simple.
A little onion,
and applesauce, of course,
but basically,
it's potatoes and grease.
She brought them to the table,
perfectly crisp and hot,
three at a time.
Oh that mother martyr bit—
kitchen door shut,
window wide open
to the winter-cold air,
knuckles bleeding into
the blue enameled bowl,
burn marks from oil splatters.
How come I can grate potatoes
without injury
and fry pancakes
in several skillets so all
can eat together?
Are mine therefore inferior?
She can have the laurel,
as in singing and sewing.
That's not what our
competition is about.
It's about who
can live longest with grief.

My medicine is
two measures of brandy,
one for the grease
and one for the grief.

The Curse of Potato Dumplings

Look up dumplings
in any German cookbook
and you may find
as many as forty listings,
from apple to farina,
liver to marrow,
plus at least
three basic versions
of potato dumplings:
raw, cooked, half and half.
Even with the most detailed recipe,
there is always the risk that
after all the weighing
grating mashing and forming
they might just fall apart
when gently lowered
into the boiling water or stock.
My mother, married
into a family of renowned cooks,
never overcame her fear of failure.
When she discovered
the first convenience food
ever marketed in Germany,
a potato dumpling mix
called *Pfanni,* I watched her
pour the contents of the box
into water and produce
six perfect globes
pronounced excellent
by my father at the dinner table.

And I, in my nine-year-old
righteousness, said: Especially
considering they are made
from a packet.

My life-long punishment
for that traitorous remark,
my punishment and shameful secret
as the heir to the famous cooking gene:
I lust for my mother's dumplings in a box,
now even more conveniently packaged
in little pouches.
Will I ever be absolved
of this guilty craving?
Do I want to be?

Made in Germany

Among the many
lovingly wrapped presents
in the birthday package
were twelve plastic clothespins
in the shape of little bears,
four yellow,
four orange,
four blue,
delicate enough
for underwear
or handkerchiefs.
They were labeled
bombenfest, bombproof.
Imagine that.

Dresden, 1945

The petrified angel looks down
on the doomsday devastation
the field of rubble
the grey wasteland
habitations mutated
to charnel houses
cellars to catacombs
the whole town
a debris-filled tumulus.
Only the cathedral
although damaged
still stands
gargoyles grinning
and the helpless angel
cleaving to its parapet
pitying the living and the dead
the dust and the ashes.

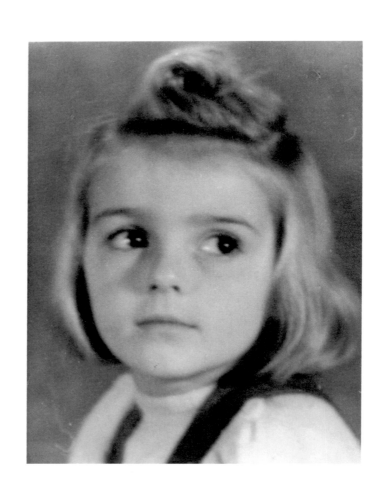

Endtime

I. Entitled

As an aristocrat
I would be my lady.
As a commoner
I was Miss, Mrs. & Ms.
As an academic
I am Master of Arts.

One art I practice
with perspicacity
is creating titles,
not for myself but for
lectures, poems & books.

Another art is that
of letting go:
I passed on titles
to two loved houses
& the only title left
is to a plot
at Greenwood Cemetery.

II. Embedded

Once upon a war the stork left his chimney nest
just before it was bombed
and dropped the baby in a laundry basket.

On her first birthday ration cards
provided a crib; in her second year
the crib was buried under rubble.

Now the girl slept womb-warm with her mother
in the narrow bed of
white damask, red cherrywood, and black ebony.

After seven years the father came home
from Cossack country
and she had to sleep on a cot
at the foot of her parents' bed.

Upon leaving childhood behind
without a trail of pebbles or crumbs
she tried out many more than the seven
dwarves' beds and always slept well
undisturbed by sags hardness or peas.

In her third decade she cleared the briars
around her first house and bought her first bed
of plain brass already patined by
love and birth and death.

At threescore and ten
she handed down the double brass bed
as a bridal gift and set out
searching for her last bed,
also her cradle her crib and her coffin.

When she found the bed that was meant for her
she had to ransom it from the wrongful
possession of a heartless innkeeper
before she could bring it home—
her fairy bed
standing free
in the middle of her chamber
bedecked with enough white linen and muslin
to set sail like a ship
enough plumage and down
to take wing like a bird.

III. Encoded

Buried under layers of accretion
the old patterns emerge
with the solace of familiarity
as I revise my life one more time:

Apartment living a homecoming
rung in by the bottom doorbell,
reminder of childhood pranks.
Two stairs up, the door opens
to a recognizable configuration
of three rooms, a small kitchen,
and the quintessential balcony
where sweet peas, geraniums and herbs
compete with the view
and weekly wash
festoons the drying rack.

Daily walks to the library,
post office, shops,
to farmers' markets and grocery,
filling my mother's wicker basket.

The week punctuated by
Sunday church with the old hymns,
Friday fish from the fishmonger,
Saturday bread from the bakery,
and favorite radio programs—
dancing with Strauss,
gladdened by Mozart,
saddened by Brahms.

Ample time again
for hikes in the forest
singing of wanderlust,
for reading and writing,
postprandial naps, for
counting the clock's melodious chimes
and frequent visits
to the cemetery where I enact
what I used to watch,
the fussing with flowers
and conversations with the dead,
the last and least expected ritual
to come home to.

Lullabies

My mother's pure soprano
seduced me to sleep
no matter what the words
or the surroundings, in the bedroom
or in the bombshelter
during air-raids where
she used up her whole repertory.
I still know all the melodies
but not all the verses. Now and then,
late in the day, songbook
in my lap, lost love and trust
on my mind, I pick through
the familiar favorites: flowers
sleeping in the moonlight,
nodding on their stems, birds
tucked into their nests, God
knowing the number of stars
upon the heavenly tent
as well as the number and names
of all cherished children.
Some lullabies end as
a sung prayer with ambiguity
between a night's rest
            and eternal rest.

When I serenaded my dear departed
at the cemetery
with Brahms' lullaby,

Guten Abend, gut' Nacht!
Mit Rosen bedacht,
mit Näglein besteckt,
schlupf unter die Deck' !
Morgen früh, wenn Gott will,
wirst du wieder geweckt,
morgen früh, wenn Gott will,
wirst du wieder geweckt.

I walked away with satisfaction
for having reached
my mother's high notes.

Nunc dimittis

if only I knew
what you looked at last
welcoming your death
in the room tidied
for departure

the empty rectangle
on the wall where
my picture used to hang

or the white expanse
of unsullied ceiling
for sketching
hieroglyphic memories

or the turning black disc
decoding the wonder
of Mozart's flute concerto

or the red geraniums
in windowboxes
the blue sky beyond
and (please, God!)
a passing bird or two

Lamentation

One ocean and one continent
deemed a sufficient degree
    of separation,
naturalization a welcoming
name for a stultifying
ceremony—
    hand on my heart
not for the country
(not for another fatherland)
but for My Land,
twenty acres of the Beautiful
between the Columbia
and the Pacific
where I defuse fears
(helicopters are not airplanes).

My history's history
haunting me
like original sin—
the war is ubiquitous,
the war owns me,
the Columbia rolls on
after passing Hanford
where the bomb was made
that fell on Nagasaki,

the Pacific is misnamed—
here, too, thousands
were herded into camps,
Japanese not Jews—
here, too, a submarine
surfaced close to the shore

and fired—
here, too, a bomb killed
a pregnant woman and five children,
        a paper balloon bomb,
one of many hand-made by girls,
carried across the ocean
on the wind from Japan—

here, too, is home now
(where else would I go?)
still adding to my litany
of lamentation,
taking the weight
which I cannot and must not
put down
to the river, to the ocean
(it's not the water's fault
        nor the wind's)
to the forests surrounding the forts:
among the trees
there is levity
                Oh Beautiful!

The Holiness of Broken Things

In the sculptures of this collection, the intent is to achieve the look of something long buried that shows that natural forces have shaped the piece as much as the human hand: an ossuary found among Roman ruins or a reliquary salvaged from a medieval shipwreck, objects that suggest ancient rituals and mysterious purposes. Some are reliquaries for housing the remains of things we hold dear while others are imaginary containers for capturing emotions or sentiments that can't be housed.

Charles Schweigert

of once rusty scrap metal
transformed by faith in beauty

In Pledge

(Offering Plate)

from my emptiness
      lostness
      sadness
from my brokenness
      littleness
      and poorness

I lift up this receptacle
      to the fullness
           of Your grace

Ossuary

    reliquaries
    sarcophagi
    coffins
    urns
containers for the dead
        whole bodies
        holy parts of bodies
        ashes

an ossuary
holds solely bones
last to decay in the ground
least to burn at cremation

where was poor Yorick taken
after the gravedigger and Hamlet
had soliloquized over his skull?
to the churchyard's
        ossuary
awaiting the last trump

Saint Sebastian

(Reliquary for St. Sebastian)

not the naked body
of a pretty boy
studded with arrows
where blood flows

but a portable reliquary
to own and carry home
for contemplation of wounds
that do not bleed red

toy arrows piercing
the casket of wire
wound and bound
footed on silver skeins

the arrow of arrogance
the arrow of rejection
the arrow of betrayal
the arrow of complacency
the arrow of condescension
the arrow of intolerance

trust to open the lid
and reveal the hidden
immutable target
filament pendant
of the forgiving heart

The Monstrance of Hildegard
(Monstrance for Hildegard von Bingen)

musician   mystic

visionary   abbess

theologian   illuminator

feather
on the breath
of God

fire
from the furnace
of faith

scientist   healer

preacher   epistler

poet   sister

Overstory: Zero

(Reliquary of the Last Tree)

arbor vitae
tree of life
This we have known of old as sacred:
    how peaceful the olive
    how strong the oak
    how victorious the palm
    how proud the laurel
    how sweet the linden.

arbor irae
tree of strife
This we have known of old as cursed:
    how tempting the tree of knowledge
        for Adam and Eve
    how irresistible the felling
    of the cedars of Lebanon
        for Gilgamesh
    how irreversible the clearcutting
    of forests from Apennine to Amazon
        for all the world.

When there is
no canopy of foliage left,
the industry's inventory notes
    overstory: zero.

59

Saint George
(Reliquary for St. George and the Dragon)

Where is your white steed
and your banner so bold?
your tasseled reins
and your cuirass of gold?
    Sainted soldier
    ancient legend
    knight of the sad countenance—
there are rulers still
who think nothing
of sacrificing
young lives as dragon fodder.
Take up the old cause again,
never mind the obsolete armor
piecemeal chain mail
and remains of trophies.
Shine up your halo, but
let the lance
rest and rust.
        Fight
as warrior of word and wisdom,
you and your dragon,
be champions of peace now!

The Holiness of Broken Things
(Reliquary for St. Catherine of Alexandria)

the base is the ark
where Noah cradled all creatures
the base is the barque
where Christ slept through the storm
anchoring a broken orb
of once rusty scrap metal
transformed by faith in beauty
the martyr's wheel rises
the break beatified
by a fragmented halo
silvery traces of the soul's flight
        toward paradise
leaving behind
        for our solace
a delicate blue flower
        love-in-a-mist

Saint John the Baptist
(Reliquary for St. John the Baptist)

in the wilderness
he prepared himself
for his arduous charge
in the desert
he smelted his essence
into a body
indistinguishable
from the hides
that clothed him
a bark-brown apparition
    resonating
with the foretelling message

Saint Brendan
(Reliquary for St. Brendan the Navigator)

Take me along
on the cloud-boat journey
to your destiny's
    destination
in storm and calm assured
by God's compass
and the spirit's breath.

I want to be aboard
all berthed in blue
when the sail billows
toward truth and peace
perhaps in Innisfree
or on the fairway to
    Finisterre—

The Burning Bush
(Chalice of the Burning Bush)

At first, Moses
was mostly
    curious:
a fire spontaneously ignited
a fire not consuming its fuel
a fire without heat
and without ashes?

    When the Voice
from within the conflagration
called him by his name,
Moses was
    awe-struck
    and hid his face
even before
the Voice tasked him
with unwanted leadership.

The sheep, meanwhile,
keep on grazing,
indifferent to
    theophany
which all seekers
    pray for, and fear.

Chalice of Tears
(Chalice for the Shedding of Tears)

The psalmist says
  "You have noted
  my lamentation;
  put my tears
  into your bottle;
  are they not recorded
  in your book?"
But oh, the woes
of our world are
too numerous and far-flung
for a bottle's finite measure
or the confines of a book.
It's not just my own grief,
there are

              sorrows
communal, national, global,
vast enough to cause
unceasing weeping.
So let us shed
our individual and
our collective tears
into a porous bowl
to be contained
     as shapes
     as shadows
     as echoes
     as habitable grief.

Learning to Beg

(Beggar's Bowl)

Every pilgrim
       is a mendicant
even if she carries
a credit card in her bosom
having little faith in
God's largesse.

      Paradoxically,
with each additional
unexpected gift
her burden lightens
as her beggar's bowl
fills with radiance
lasting a lifetime.

Karin Giesecke Temple

child of war
*
emigrant
*
teacher
*
farmer
*
poet
*
pilgrim

I am indebted to the *Psalms,* Nelly Sachs, Paul Celan, Bertolt Brecht, Carolyn Forché, Eavan Boland, Mary Oliver, Kenneth Helphand, Kathleen Flenniken, and Nancy Nowak, and grateful for the encouragement of Jim Dott, Birgit Feld-Raetzer, Jörg Carlsson, and Cheryl Silverblatt.

At the original 2015 showing of North Oregon Coast artist Charles Schweigert's sculptures at RiverSea Galley in Astoria, Karin Temple read the accompanying sequence of poems, which were also displayed alongside the sculptures.

Other books by Karin Temple:

Child of War
weimar X 2 (with Lucien Swerdloff)
Peregrina
In the Company of Saints (with Christi Payne)
So Great a Cloud of Witnesses (with Christi Payne)

Designed by Greg Darms at the floating hut studio, in the winter-into-spring season of sparrow song and daffodil emergence. Typeset in ITC New Baskerville, designed by John Baskerville in England in the 1750s.

CPSIA information can be obtained at www.ICGtesting.com
Printed in the USA
BVIW12n0931270316
441827BV00002B/3